Guess Who's in the
Trees

Picture credits
(t=top, b=bottom, l=left, r=right, c=center, fc=front cover)
FLPA: 4–5 Jules Cox; 8–9 IMAGEBROKER, WINFRIED SCHÄ¤FER;
10–11 Martin Van Lokven/Minden Pictures; 14–15 Derek Middleton; 16–17 Hugh Lansdown
Getty: 6–7 J & C Sohns
Shutterstock: fc, 3 Dirk Ercken; 12–13 Cathy Keifer; 18–19 KAMONRAT

Editor: Ruth Symons
Cover Designer: Krina Patel
Editorial Director: Victoria Garrard
Art Director: Laura Roberts-Jensen

Copyright © QEB Publishing 2014

First published in the United States by
QEB Publishing, Inc. 3 Wrigley,
Suite A, Irvine, CA 92618

www.qed-publishing.co.uk

A CIP record for this book is available from the Library of Congress.

ISBN 978 1 60992 706 6

Printed in China

Guess Who's in the Trees

Camilla De La Bédoyère and Fiona Hajée

QEB Publishing

Who sleeps in a treetop nest?

Who buries nuts and seeds in the ground?

Who has a
fluffy red tail?

I do!

I am a red squirrel.

It is hard to find food in winter, so I must find some now and hide it for later.

Who has eyes that look two ways at once?

Who flies around
the treetops?

Who has babies
called caterpillars?

Who has bright, spotty wings?

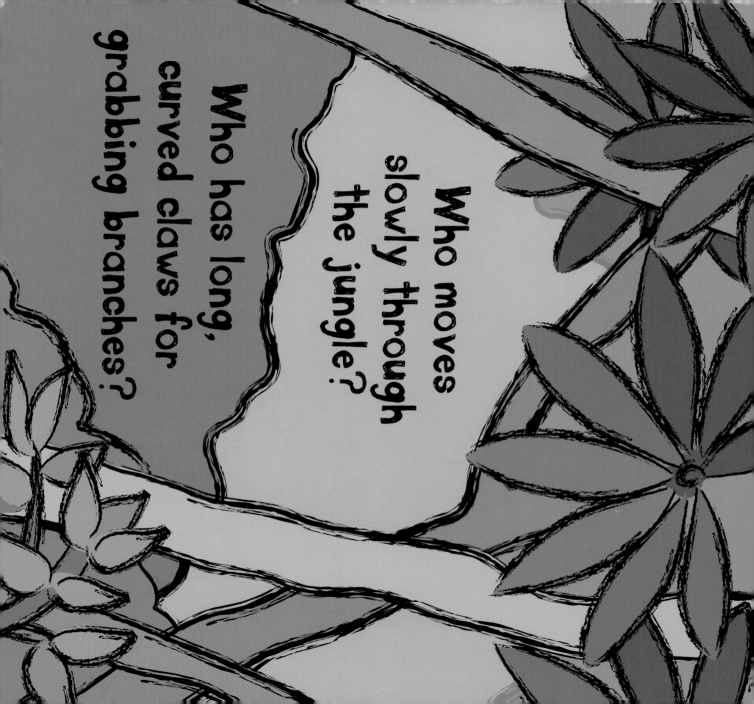

Who hangs
upside down?

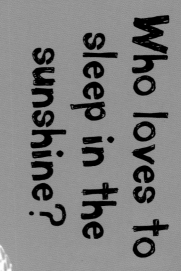

Who loves to
sleep in the
sunshine?

Who has dry, scaly skin?

Who hisses and slithers?

I climb trees to find
animals to eat. I wrap my
coils around them and
squeeeeeze tight!

I do!

I am a snake.

Talking points

1. The first time you read the book with your child, encourage them to guess the identity of each animal before turning the flap. Talk together about how they guessed the animal's identity. Did they look at the picture, listen to the words, or use both sets of clues?

2. Go on a nature trek to find out which trees grow near you. Collect leaves, seeds, flowers, or nuts from the ground. At home, these items can be stuck to sheets of paper and used to identify the types of tree.

3. On the nature trek, look for any animals that live in or near the trees. Teach your child the importance of respecting habitats and the animals that live in them, and how to observe nature safely.

4. Rain forests are a very special habitat. Use the Internet or books to find out more about them: Where are they, and what animals live there?